Demetria Buie

Ms. CEO/Founder/ EDITOR-IN-CHIEF Of EMPOWERING Women To Speak Out Magazine. Founded in 2014

First and foremost; Demetria Buie is a dedicated, loving mother to her son. Buie, despite being an accomplished entrepreneur, holds her title as 'mother' most dear to her heart. As a youth, she faced her fair share of challenges. Buie dropped out of junior high school and ultimately left her small town in Louisiana at eighteen years old and moved to Richmond, Virginia. Despite dropping out of school, she never gave up. Buie received her GED at twenty three and then pursued an acting degree at John Tyler Community College. She then obtained employment after college but was left unfulfilled by the work she was doing. As a result, she walked off of her job in 2013 and has yet to look back. She has transformed her life and become a well reputed entrepreneur in her community.

Buie is an accomplished author (37 published books), publisher, business owner, Magazine owner, life-story coach, and renowned international speaker. She was recently named 2018 Female Entrepreneur of the Year. Her success stems from her innate mindset of transforming obstacles into opportunities. Buie's road to success was full of difficulties. At one point, she found herself homeless, depressed, and suicidal. It was at this point that Buie learned to reconstruct her pain into passion. She began writing her first book, an autobiography, titled Refuse to Lose in 2009. Her newly found optimism and

1

relentless pursuit of Christ reignited her spirit. Buie found purpose, motivation, and hope for a better future. Realizing that her past did not have to define her future, she knew she was destined for bigger and better things. Buie decided to dedicate her time to helping others and empowering those who have been dealt a rough hand, especially women. Empowering others is how Buie makes a difference in the lives of others. She recently hosted her first "Empowerment Brunch" to inspire women. Her speaking abilities and authentic experiences captivate any audience she speaks before. Buie now laughs in the face of adversity, and works tirelessly to help others achieve the same mindset.

"We cannot change the events that have occurred in our past – in some instances, we may not have had much choice in them, but we do have the power to create our future" I Refuse To Lose.

–Demetria Buie

Ramona is the CEO & Lead Designer of V and T Events. She specializes in curating unique designs, lavish floral and personalized planning. Her passion is exemplified in her work and in her relationship with each client. She lives in Northwest Florida, primarily serves the Emerald Coast, and has traveled to multiple location throughout the Unites States. Her mother Victoria introduced her to the Industry at a young age, but it was not until she was asked to plan her first wedding at Eglin Air Force Base, she realized her true passion and love for designing!

Ramona then honed her talent while working for the base general in protocol. She learned all she could on the proper techniques and etiquette for creating lavish events for distinguished guest and dignitaries. After the military, V and T Events was established and Ramona has been Creating Forever Beautiful Memories for her clients ever since. Living in Florida has a given her the opportunity to work with different cultures from across the world as they experienced her first class planning for their destination weddings. She has had the honor of also serving The Elite United States Blue Angles, world class athletes, actors and many others distinguished professional leader.

Ramona is highly active in her community and love to support the youth. She donates her time and funds to support Battled Women and Children, and mentoring young women. Her faith and family mean the world to her so when she is not designing this is where she spends her time.

Ramona
CEO & Lead Designer of V and T Events LLC

Dare To Dream!

LEXUS

Alexis is taking the esthetician world by storm in Monroe, Louisiana. She is your one-stop for all things beauty and business. While she is heavily sought after for her lash and near pain-free Brazilian services, she has an arsenal of services that are blazing trails of their own. One of the more popular services is her advanced skincare for teens, women, and men. Her warm smile and personality greets each client at the first consultation and instantly puts you at ease.

There are no such things as strangers as all leave feels like family within seconds of being in the salon. Clients realize quickly that they are not coming in for just some soap and water affair. Alexis thoroughly explains all products and their benefits then offers a brief synopsis of what they can expect to ensure that clients are comfortable and leave more in tune with their skin. Alexis has 8 years of experience in perfecting the skin of all types and producing instant results. Her signature facial service is Viral Facebook Facial with derma planing and her clients are raving about the effects weeks later.

The list of services also includes body sculpting and contouring for those looking for non-surgical methods to add a little spice to their figure. The atmosphere, the customer service, and the quality of the services have landed her amongst the Top 3 in her area, and on the local news station KTVE 10. This is only the beginning and Alexis is proving such as she continues to refine her craft through continuing education and innovation.

Alexis Cherrell Hollistic & Wellness Spa
1501 Arkansas Ave Monroe, La 71201
Vagaro.com/Essentialvanitysalon
Alexischerrell.site

Fashion 101

Fashion is a way of introducing yourself without having to say a word.

What's In Your Closet?

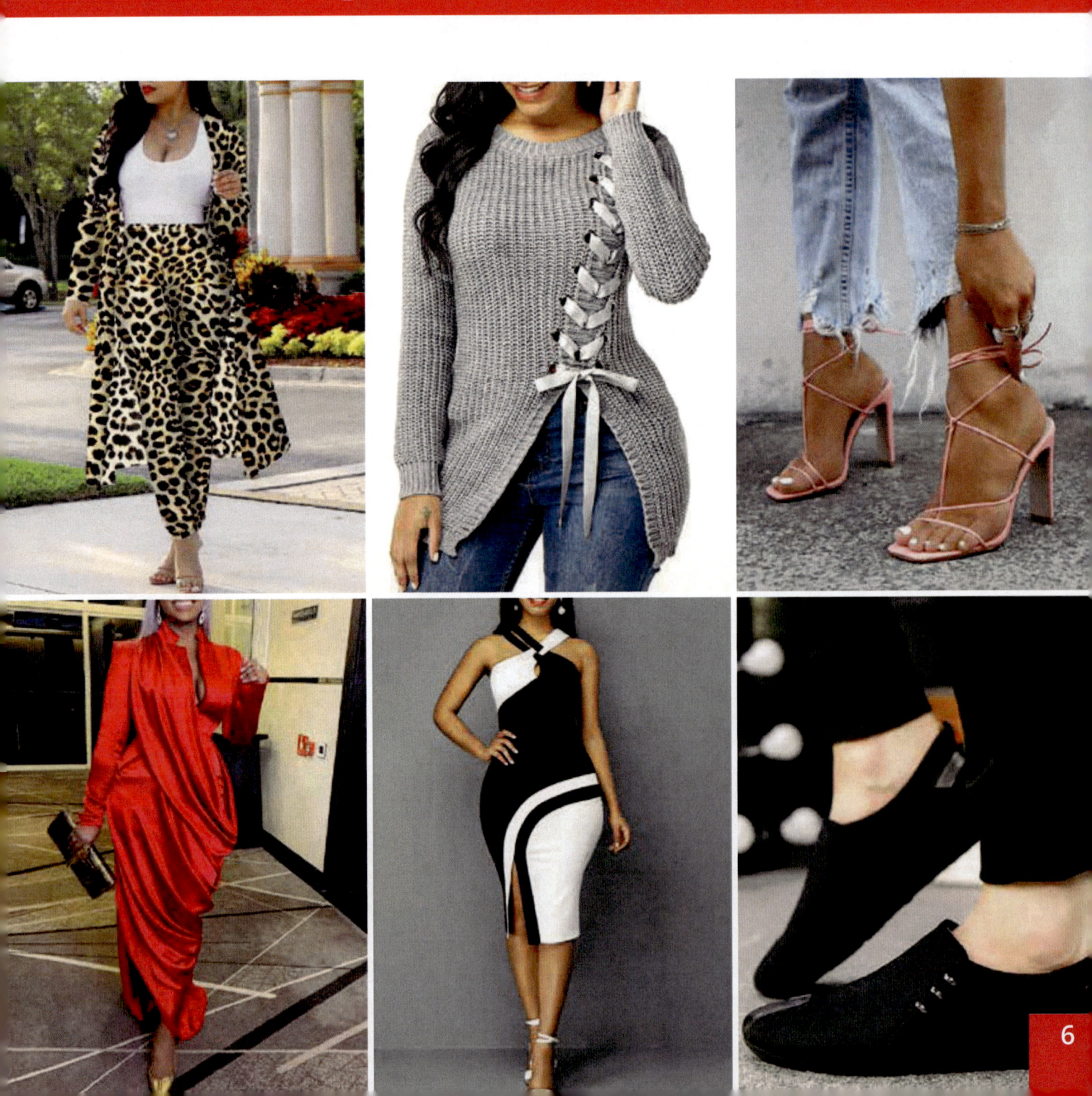

Creamy Chocolate
SEX IN A PAN
keto - low carb - sugar free

TOOLS TO MAKE SEX IN A PAN DESSERT:

9×9 baking dish – This is the one I used.
Medium saucepan – This one is a good size if you're making the old version of the chocolate layer.
Hand mixer – For beating the whipped cream.
Sugar-free dark chocolate – This one is sweetened with stevia. Don't confuse it with unsweetened baking chocolate!

Course Dessert | Cuisine American
Calories 344 kcal, Prep Time 20 minutes, Cook Time 25 minutes, Total Time 45 minutes

Chocolate Layer - (old version, like pudding)

While the crust is cooling, make the chocolate pudding layer. In a medium saucepan, combine the heavy cream, almond milk, sugar-free dark chocolate, butter, and powdered erythritol. Cook over medium-low to low heat, stirring frequently, until the chocolate is melted and sweetener dissolves (about 5-10 minutes). Be careful not to get the heat too high to avoid burning the chocolate.

Gradually sprinkle the xanthan gum into the saucepan a little at a time (don't just dump it in) and immediately whisk to incorporate. Continue to heat for about 5 minutes, whisking constantly. Remove from heat, then whisk in the vanilla extract.

Cool the chocolate pudding for 15 minutes (it will thicken, but still be liquid). You can add more xanthan gum if needed, but don't add too much or it will get slimy. Stir/whisk again after cooling, then pour it over the cream cheese layer.

Cover with plastic wrap, making sure it's directly against the surface to prevent a film forming. Refrigerate for at least.

Whipped Cream Layer

Use a hand mixer to beat the cream, vanilla extract, and powdered erythritol together, until stiff peaks form.

Spread the whipped cream over the chocolate layer. Sprinkle chocolate shavings on top.

Refrigerate for 1-2 more hours (or as long as needed until serving) to fully set.

Black Girls Rock

2021. Legacy

Demetria Buie
Visionary/Founder
Mentor. Speaker. Author. Event Host.
Magazine Owner

Anika Cohen
Dover, DE
I create strategy, solutions & success to propel forward with clarity and confidence.

Shamekia Bryant
Monroe LA
Herbal Medicine

Aretha Ford-Metts
Cincinnati, Ohio
Podcaster of MisHandled

Dr. Sharon H. Porter
Maryland
Publisher

Cynthia Robinson
Newark, New Jersey
Self Love Specialist

Dr. Tarama Lashay Fleming
Dothan, Alabama
Licensed Professional Counselor/
Owner, A Clear View Counseling
Services, LLC

Pamela Tate
Louisiana
Author/Speaker

Dr. Fayola Delica
Miami, FL
Passion and Purpose Activator

Gwen Finley
Richmond, Virginia
Author & Speaker

Monique Tucker
Monroe, Louisiana
Author & Speaker

Nomvula Rakolote
South Africa
Speaker, Mentor

Dr. Alvetta Green
South Carolina
Speaker & Author

Dr. Kishma George
Delaware
Author & Evangelist

Quinn Conyers
Maryland
Entrepreneur & Author

Monique A.J Smith
Hampton Virginia
Sports Administration

Elect Lady Casty Jones
Jonesville NC
CEO of 2 Businesses Divine Boutique & Accessories, CastyJewelry

Aline Mays-Easley
Alabama
Mental Health Therapist & Author

Prophetess Natisha Wilson

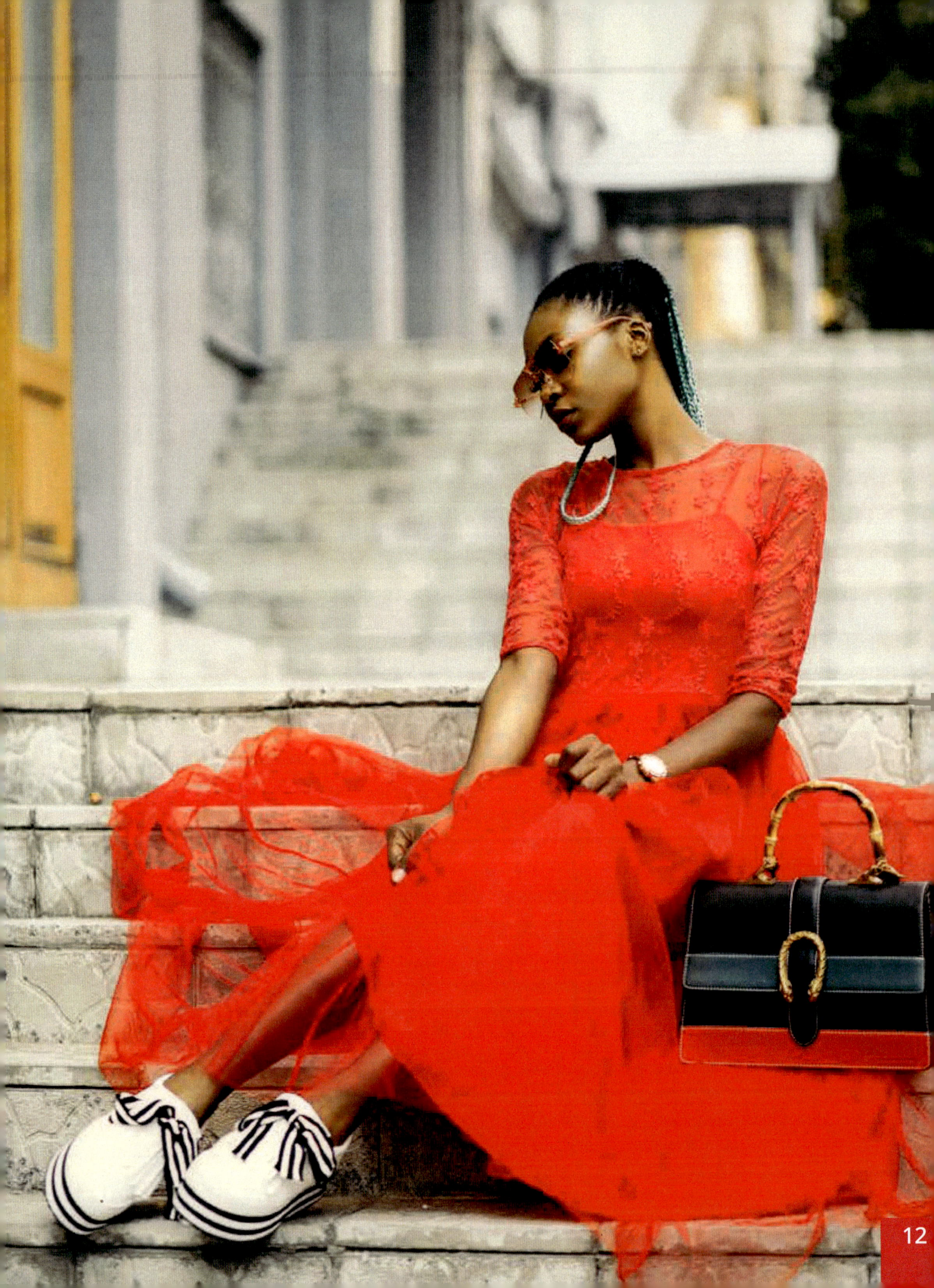

Being in Love Again During the Holidays

Beatrice Tucker

Being in Love can definitely be an amazing experience especially during the holidays. The holidays are usually a time of family gatherings, delicious food, and lots of tradition. It's the time that we reflect on our lives and vow to change things that may have not worked for us during the year. The holidays can also be a time of loneliness and sadness for so many this was a place that I found myself in before I met my soulmate and yes, I said soulmate. I can remember a time I completely dreaded but I would push myself to get through them, I then realized that I was missing the point and that one day I would love again during the holidays. While I waited, I begin to apply the same principal that I seen work in every area of my life I begin using Love affirmations to encourage myself while I waited. Affirmation are short positive statements that change your perspective and encourage you here are some of the affirmation I would say daily during my season of waiting for Love again during the holidays. You will love aging hold fast to your dreams and empty your hands from any past hurts so that God can fill them.

Love Affirmations

- All I see is love.
- In life I always get what I give, and I always give out love.
- My heart is always open to love.
- Everywhere I go, I find love. Life is joyous.
- Love shines from within me.
- I am grateful for the love that is around me.
- I am attracted to love.
- I am a loving person.
- I am Worthy of love.
- I will choose love over fear.
- I am a magnet for love.
- Holiday love is the best love.
- I am grateful for the ability to love.
- I will open my heart to love
- I am passionate and inspired and full of love.
- I have love to share inside of me.
- I will attract my soulmate.
- My soulmate will find me, and we will live happily ever after.

- BEATRICE MONIUQE also known as BEA is an entrepreneur, minster, motivation speaker, and business coach. Her mission is to empower those called into the marketplace to Bea great and walk in purpose. She empowers, coaches and mentor business owners to operate their business with kingdom principles and marketplace strategies that have propelled them to the top. BEATRICE MONIQUE has reached and motivated countless business owners to dream again. With over 17 years of experience in every aspect of business, from management to ownership, it is obvious why many choose her as their business coach. Her straightforward approach and infectious energy give entrepreneurs the push they need to manifest their dreams. Beatrice serves in ministry and is the founder of Cracked Vessel Ministries. This ministry encourages women to live pass the hurt and allow God to fill them with his love. Without a doubt you can expect to see this name more in the future. She is also the owner of ABA Billing Solutions which is a medical billing and consulting firm that serves practices all over the country. She is the Author of BEA GREAT & Mind Your Business a book that focuses on renewing the mind of all entrepreneurs. She is also the CEO and founder of Kingdom Streetz Consulting this company focus is empowering ministers to become business owners and network in the kingdom of God. Beatrice currently resides in Monroe, Louisiana.

- Website: www.icanbeagreat.com
- Facebook: @icanbeagreat2
- Email:Kingdomstreetzconsulting@gmail.com

Stay Connected!!!

Happy Empowerment

Here are 7 Tips for 2021.

1. Start embracing your humanness and giving yourself more credit.
2. Start making your own happiness a priority.
3. Start putting your heart and soul into the things you do.
4. Start taking more deep breaths, so you can mindfully collect more lessons for the year ahead.
5. Start paying more attention to the right people.
6. Start Talking to God more about things you feel is embarrassing.
7. Start forgiving yourself and others.

TODAY is the beginning. Let there be no excuses, no explanations, and no regrets this holiday season. When you THINK BETTER about yourself and your present opportunities, you LIVE BETTER despite the challenges you face.

- Demetria Buie Ministries

www.demetriaministries.com
Subscribe NOW to our Empowerment 2021 issues.
www.buiemagazines.com

16

Jason N. Linton

Born in New York City on October 29th, 1970, Jason N. Linton served in the US Navy and now lives in Simpsonville, South Carolina. Jason & his wife Alisha were married on February 7th, 2009. They enjoy having a blended family consisting of five daughters, two granddaughters and two grandsons.

Jason is a certified life coach, cognitive behavior therapist and serves as an ordained elder. Jason is also the author of the relationship rollercoaster entitled "Love, Torcha" and relationship reality check called "Uncomplicate it". Jason founded the mentorship program "Manifestation" that helps men and woman of all ages heal, grow, and become free from past failures and offenses.

Jason and his wife also lead a marriage ministry his wife called "The Linton Bridge" which empowers couples to identify and address areas that interfere with achieving their best relationship/marriage.

Three reason marriages end in divorce

For years, the percentage of marriages that end in divorce remained in the neighborhood of fifty percent. While some recent reports show the number of divorces has slightly decreased, it's duly noted the number of couples getting married has slightly decreased as well. Whether these numbers increase or decrease, here are three reason marriages end in divorce.

#1) Foundational Structure

Many couples enter marriage lacking a blueprint for marriage. At the foundation, there has to be four pillars to build upon. These pillars are love, faith, vision, and work. Similar to an onion, each pillar has many layers which are bound to bring tears to the eyes of any committed couple. Without the support of healthy communication, intentional comprehension and constant appreciation, divorce can easily become an attractive escape hatch from a collapsing relationship. Unfortunately, roughly one out of two couples who reach a breaking point and will reach for the escape hatch rather than reach out for relationship counseling because of the mental, emotional, and physical wear and tear of the relationship.

#2) Marriage is not profitable

The attack on marriages has reached an all-time high. Divorce, broken families and independence are all big business. The three headed monster, (Hollywood, social media and the music industry) make it hard to find and hard to become a happy, healthy and honorable marriage. It is increasingly difficult for a couple to go against the grain of popular opinion and profitable agendas, when the couple was not modeled a healthy marriage as a child. Over time, the external influences begin chipping away at the relationship's support system and eventually suffocate the oxygen within the relationship. When couples reach the point of simply trying to survive, divorce becomes a strong option to breathe again.

#3) Relationship Taxes

Every relationship/marriages involves relationship taxes. Whether these taxes stem from our parents or previous relationships, these taxes will be paid by our current partner. The good news is, these taxes can drive away Mr. / Mrs. Wrong, but the bad news is these taxes can also take a toll on a person capable of spending a lifetime with. The key is to appreciate the one graced to deal with your good, bad ugly and beautiful. Once someone feels unappreciated, they will look for places and people who will appreciate them. This is how affairs many affairs happen and divorce becomes the end result.

18

Monique S Clark

    Monique S Clark a Certified success life Coach and entrepreneur with over 15 years of experience, she graduated with a Degree in Business Administration. While in college Monique started her first workshops for Life skills, Financial Literacy and Entrepreneurship. She continues her passion by receiving a Certification in Community Financial Empowerment, became a Certified Facilitator for National Programs Strengthening Families and Getting Ahead.

Monique is the proud owner of Success with Monique; the goal is to help "Bridge the Gap of Today's Economy with Practical Skills while promoting Self-Sufficiency focusing on low-income communities with programs and workshops. " . A mental health advocate (QMHS) and Community Health Worker with MBHG. A network marketing Professional for over 3 years.

Owner of Success with Monique coaches' clients to become successful in many areas of their lives from personal to business.

She is also the founder of the Kurvology Brand Kurvology is a movement to help promote self-love and build confidence in kurvy women and girls through modeling, pageants, events and fashion.

Monique has over 10 years of modeling and print experience. Kurvology models have been featured in Micah Steven Fashion Week, Ohio Fashion Week and hosted a Kurvy Girl Pageant.

Kurvology' Boutique was launched in November 2020 and will feature runway looks and is dedicated to helping women find the right shapewear and clothing to fit their right body types.

Kurvology's mission is to provide fashionable, affordable and comfortable shapewear and clothing for kurvy women of all sizes.

Loneliness is a valid feeling

Do you crave a connection?

Do you like being alone but at the same time you hate being alone?

Loneliness does not make you weak!!

These are my Top 10 Self-Care ideas to not feel lonely?

1. Find out why you are lonely? is it because? ask yourself.
2. Do not listen to the negative inner voice -tell yourself something positive. Try I'AM statements every day.
3. Date yourself -learn more about what you like. Plan a date night out or a date night in alone or with friends.
4. Treat Yourself to a spa day -get pampered for once or twice.
5. Check into a hotel for a staycation or take a solo trip for you.
6. Accept you deserve the best -Never Settle
7. Do a photoshoot -find your alter ego
8. Dance like no one is watching- star in your own music video
9. Cook your favorite dishes or even try cooking something new
10. If you need support do not be afraid to reach out !! for professional help

Hope theses 10 Ideas Can Help You Not Feel Lonely This Season!!!

Minister Lina Lassiter

Advanced Grief Recovery Method Specialist
Founder and President, Forever Healed

Lina Lassiter is a Senior Manager on the claim's eligibility team at Genworth Financial. She has over 20 years of insurance industry experience, including auto, general liability, risk management and worker's compensation. She holds a Bachelor's degree in Business Management, with a concentration in Leadership. Lina has also earned certifications in Grief Recovery and Crisis Intervention. Lina is also pursuing a Master's degree in Human Services Counseling with a concentration in PTSD, Trauma and Grief.

Lina is Founder and President of Forever Healed, a 501c3 non-profit whose vision is to continually help people recover from the impact of death, divorce, and other losses and to help them bridge the gap between the feelings of despair and healing. In this capacity, Lina facilitates grief recovery classes (1:1 and group sessions) in a nurturing and safe environment, as well as provides the tools needed for recovery: to those dealing with incomplete emotions to include anxiety and depression due to a death, divorce or other loss. The non-profit also offers after school grief sessions to administrators, educators, and school counselors. They also provide grief and mentoring sessions to children who are dealing with feelings of despair and depression as a result of a loss (divorce, death, incarcerated parent, bullying).

Lina has presented The Hidden Cost of Grief presentation in the workplace to military personnel, corporate organizations, and churches. Her civic participation within the Richmond community, includes overseeing the youth ministry, and contributions to the intercessory team and ministerial staff at her church. In July 2017, Lina was licensed as a Minister of the Gospel. More recently, Lina has partnered with the Commonwealth's Attorney Office Homicide Support Group as a motivational speaker and resource to families who have endured pain and loss as a result of homicide.

Lina is passionate about assisting those grieving with overcoming their pain. After taking a grief recovery class, Lina was able to heal from years of physical, mental, and verbal abuse as a child. Lina believes that often times our condition causes us to forget our true purpose in life. In reality, our positions can change our conditions. We are fearfully and wonderfully made, even in the midst of a challenge. We should change our mindsets about being a survivor (outliving a situation) and learn to become more than conquerors in every situation by healing from the inside out.

Refuse to Lose

In order to propel forward in our careers, lives, and relationships, we must first understand what is keeping us bound. Some of us don't feel that we qualify for or deserve success. We think we must obtain additional accreditations through higher learning. Higher education is certainly warranted in a specialized field. However, confidence in your abilities and skills are the main ingredients for the win.

I was one of the first African American's to obtain a Senior Leadership position at my company, and it should be noted without a degree. I now have a degree and certifications; however, prior to obtaining my Senior Leadership position, I carried myself as a leader. I allowed my work ethics and integrity to speak louder than my voice. As such, a refuse to lose posture starts with our mindset. Understand what you bring to the table and walk in confidence.

Some of us may lack confidence as a result of negative experiences or words that have been spoken over our lives. In the past, I questioned my existence due to child abuse. I allowed soul-killing words to plague me for years. As a result, I felt my position in life was in the back of the room. I became comfortable in the back, telling myself it was humility. I understand that all people are not leaders; however, no one should be comfortable at the back of the room, take your seat at the table, own it and make change while there.

However, if you are a leader, it's time to step out. Fear will cause you to become comfortable blending in and being at the back of the room afraid of success. Some of us are wounded warriors, oblivious to the fact that our wounds keep us bound from who God called us to be. Love yourself enough to heal from past hurt and pain to better position yourself for the win.

We must understand that we are unique and individual, God's masterpiece! So, we don't fit in, we stand out regardless of position. We have been called, separated and equipped to overcome challenges and to obtain our goals. Refuse to lose, unload the baggage of self-doubt, excuses, and fear!

You got this! Refuse to lose!

Minister Lina Lassiter, Advanced Grief Recovery Method Specialist
Founder and President, Forever Healed

5 Gifts The "Boss Lady" in Your Life Would Love on Valentine's Day

Latesha is a wealth strategist, real estate investor, and CEO of Savvy Diva Enterprises in Atlanta, GA. Her company provides business consulting and financial services for small businesses.

If you're an entrepreneur, I bet you goal is to leave a legacy and generational wealth for your family. Same here! So, it's no surprise that (almost) everything that you will see on this list aligns with the goal of being financially secure. I love to receive gifts that keep on giving!

1. Real estate

The absolute best gift that my husband has ever given me is an investment property. He closed on the house as a Mother's Day gift which made it even more special. After flipping it, we sold it for a profit on my birthday. Huge brownie points for him!

2. Credit repair

Having good credit is pivotal to funding your dreams. When "life happens," many times our credit suffers due to cash flow problems. Credit repair programs can help you get back on track. The gift of excellent will pay off for years to come.

3. Paying down debt

Is there anything sexier than your significant other unexpectantly paying off a debt that you've been working to pay down? Lowering your credit utilization and debt-to-income ratio puts you in a much stronger financial position.

4. Business credit builder program

Did you know that you can build business credit under your EIN that is completely separate from your SSN? The best part is that business credit limits are typically 10 times higher than personal credit! Paying for a business credit builder program is an amazing way for bae to show their love.

5. Travel

Ok, so we can't be all about business, right? It is important to enjoy the fruits of your labor, and what better way to do that than seeing the world! (post-COVID of course) Warm sand, blue water, and fruity cocktails will put years on your marriage.

LATESHA ISBELL HOWARD

BUSINESS CREDIT & FUNDING EXPERT
REAL ESTATE INVESTOR | WEALTH STRATEGIST

Latesha is the CEO of Savvy Diva Enterprises, a consulting firm that helps small businesses to build business credit and obtain the funding they need to start or grow. An active real estate investor, Latesha also teaches her clients how to build wealth through investing in real estate.

- Lives in Atlanta with her husband Chris and 2 daughters, Akayla and Amaya
- Happily married to Chris Howard since 2008
- e-books: "5 Ways to Set Your Kids Up for Success" and "6 Secret Stages to Building Business Credit"
- President of the Board, Essence of Hope, Inc (mission to eradicate homelessness)
- Master of Business Administration B.S. in Finance
- Favorite quote: "She is clothed in strength and dignity, and she laughs without fear of the future." ~ Proverbs 31:25

Follow her day to day at

in f ⊙

25

26

The way you love yourself is the way you teach others to love you.

Now this world is full of crazy things. As we are born in mankind we are born with lots of responsibility towards our family members and towards the society. But one thing which we usually forget in this busy responsible world is that taking responsibility of self. We dependent on others for our happiness and joy. We don't feel loved until someone loves us back. Somewhere between loving others and waiting for their love in return we forgot SELF LOVE ! This life is what you are making it everyday. We are growing up and getting surrounded with so many responsibilities and feelings. These are the factors that are trapping you. Sometimes relationships affect a person in a serious way. It's not the quantity that matters its the quality. It's Okay to feel the pain sometimes. But at the end you should realize that you are individual entity and individual soul. Make your soul blissful for your self. Maslow's theory in psychology comprising a five-tier model of human needs, often depicted as hierarchical levels within a pyramid. You will find that self esteem and self actualization is depicted on the top of the prism indicating that finally as we grow up the last thing we should expect from the society is self-esteem. At the end one have to realize his/her purpose.

Here are some tips how that can be useful for

1. Fill your body with food and drink that nourishes it and makes it thrive.
2. Embrace and love the things that make you different.
3. Breathe in and out, clear your mind of your thoughts and just be.
4. Forgive yourself. You can't change the things you have done in the past but you can control your future.
5. Grab a cup of your favorite drink. The quote "Whatever happens life has to go on" is truly amazing. If you will go through a book

MAN'S SEARCH FOR MEANING

You will find that even if you are being tortured every second of the day still you can have hope. The book describes Story of a prisoner who is war camp refugee and never gave up hope even after being in worst living conditions. Also this book is recommended by great authors. Now you have to realize at least you are free. You are not one among those war camp refugees. You got to wake up every day with the sunshine and beautiful mornings. Being alive and healthy is the worthless gift we can have. Talk to yourself like you are talking someone you love. And what's the big deal if you will devote some love for yourself.

Ask yourself these questions:

1. Do you always feel you have to be in a Relationship? & Why?
2. Do you feel like you can't stand being alone or Single?
3. Is becoming a Wife your #1 Goal? If Yes, Why?

Remember: The way you love yourself is the way he will Love you!!

- **Demetria Buie**

Christy Sanderson is an Award Winning Author, Award Winning Entrepreneur of the year, and Public Speaker. She has a Bachelor's in Early Childhood Education, has a Master's in Special Education and she is an Educator!!! She has authored five other books, Woman of God Who Did God Create You To Be, From Nothing into the Woman of God: Spiritual Life, Woman of God Stop Looking for Love, God's Kingdom: Spiritual & Wealth Motivation and From Nothing into the Woman of God part 2. Christy has been featured on the cover of UBAWA Magazine, and several radio interviews. She was once a Co-Host on the Digital Breeze radio show in Atlanta, Georgia. At the young age of 23, Christy fully committed herself to God, letting Him take total control of her life, and started her own ministry, Glory Nation. Her life purpose is to experience and share God's Glory, to fulfill God's promises, and to help others become closer to Jesus Christ to find their life purpose.

7 Ways to Spend Valentine's Day Single

Valentine's Day is a very bittersweet day for me if you can believe that! First, it's my birthday, but I'm usually ALWAYS single so I have a lot of experience on how to be single on the sweetest day of the year so let's just get to it! Go out with other single friends! I'm sure you are not the only one dateless and single! Show your parents and grandparents some love. You know they love you back! Volunteer at a Senior Citizens retirement or community center. This year may be restrictive due to Covid-19, but still double check to see what they need and how you can be of service. Rent a hotel or Air B N B and just relax, binge watch your favorite movies, book a massage, order room service and simply enjoy yourself. Get a makeover, take some photos and make videos. Especially if are trying to grow your personal and professional brands. Set up a virtual Friends night. Have all of your friends invite their single friends and play "match maker". At this point someone is bound to "get lucky"! Hire a personal chef, house keeper, and any other professional services that can make your life easier for Valentines Day and beyond. Anytime you can do something to remind yourself that you deserve to be loved and happy DO IT! Valentines Day does not have to be doom and gloom just because you are single. As the late, great Whitney Houston said "Learning to love yourself is the greatest love of all"!

For More loving yourself advice please connect with me at @themoyouknow214 on Facebook, Instagram and Twitter!

Your Mobile Marketing Mogul
Www.themoyouknow.info
1-877-Mo-Knows (665-6697)
https://themoyouknow.as.me/

ShaDonna "Mo" McPhaul

Chief Executive Officer **ShaDonna McPhaul**, also known as 'Mo' is a combat veteran with 20 years of loyal service to the United States Air Force. She merged her compassion and entrepreneurial spirit and created Mo's Heroes Inc. and The Mo You Know Marketing and Media Consulting Services, LLC. As Chief Executive Officer and Founder, her vision is for Mo's Heroes to be the conduit to provide the support veterans, service members and their family members need to achieve their personal and professional goals. Mo has been featured in GI Jobs Magazine, Be Encouraged Magazine, Life in the Overflow Magazine, The Huffington Post, The State of New Office of African American Affairs Statewide Focus Magazine, Ardent for Life, the Fayetteville Observer Newspaper, Cannon Connections Newspaper, and Ho'okele Newspaper. She has been seen on ABC, NBC, CBS, and Fox. She has co-authored two best-selling books, "Shift On" and "The Voices Behind Mental Illness Anthology: The Life of a Veteran". She currently hosts "The Mo You Know" podcast where she interviews upcoming and coming entrepreneurs. She has also worked on the sales, marketing, and promotions side of radio. Mo has received several awards and recognition to include the Special Achievement Award from the NAACP-Honolulu Branch, The Mountaire Farms "Better Carolina Award, and the Values.com "Hero of the Month" for January 2015. She has also received a Certificate of Special Congressional Recognition and other special recognition awards from military leaders, elected officials and community organizations. The Department of Veterans Affair recognized Mo as "Veteran of the Day" February 2020 to kick off "Black History Month". Mo serves as the Public Image Chair for Liberty Point Rotary Club. She is the loving mother of son, Charles and a proud native of Fayetteville, North Carolina.

God is about to blow your mind!

Hey sis! God is about to blow your mind, so get ready for your supernatural blessing. It might seem like you had a hard year but every time something seems like it's going crazy in your life a major breakthrough is coming. What God has for you is for you, can't no one take that away from you. In 2020 it has been a rough year for most people but in the midst of it all, God has a plan for everything. While some people were struggling during the pandemic, others were getting blessed. God is only changing the hands of the wealth. God wants you to reach your full potential in life. Of course, He doesn't want you to be worry or have negative thoughts in life. Whatever you think, that is what you bring into your life. Start thinking positive thoughts so you can bring blessings into your life. Trust me God haven't forgotten about you, He wants to bless you like never before. He was waiting on the right time. If God can trust you with the small things, He will give you more. However, you must be thankful for what you already have. God always provides, He always come through when you least expect it. I know you're probably wondering why I'm still struggling financially? Why I'm still single, why this or why that? Let me ask you this "Do you trust God?" I mean "Do you really trust God like your life depends on it?" If you do get ready for a major breakthrough in your life because God is about to blow your mind. Everything you have been praying for is coming to pass. God will never leave you nor forsake you, God said "Come get your blessing. God loves you like crazy and He wants to give you so much more. All you must do is ask. God said "Ask and you shall receive!" This is a new beginning for you, you will no longer lose but you will receive blessings after blessings. All you have to do is have faith as small as a mustard seed. Jesus Christ said your faith will move mountains. Jesus Christ said some may even do greater works than Him. But we must have faith, be Holy and follow the Holy Spirit always. God wants to bless you like never before but He is simply waiting on you to come to Him. Because God is about to blow your mind, so go get your blessings!!!

Author
Christy Sanderson

Website: www.glorynation.org
Instagram: gracefulprincess

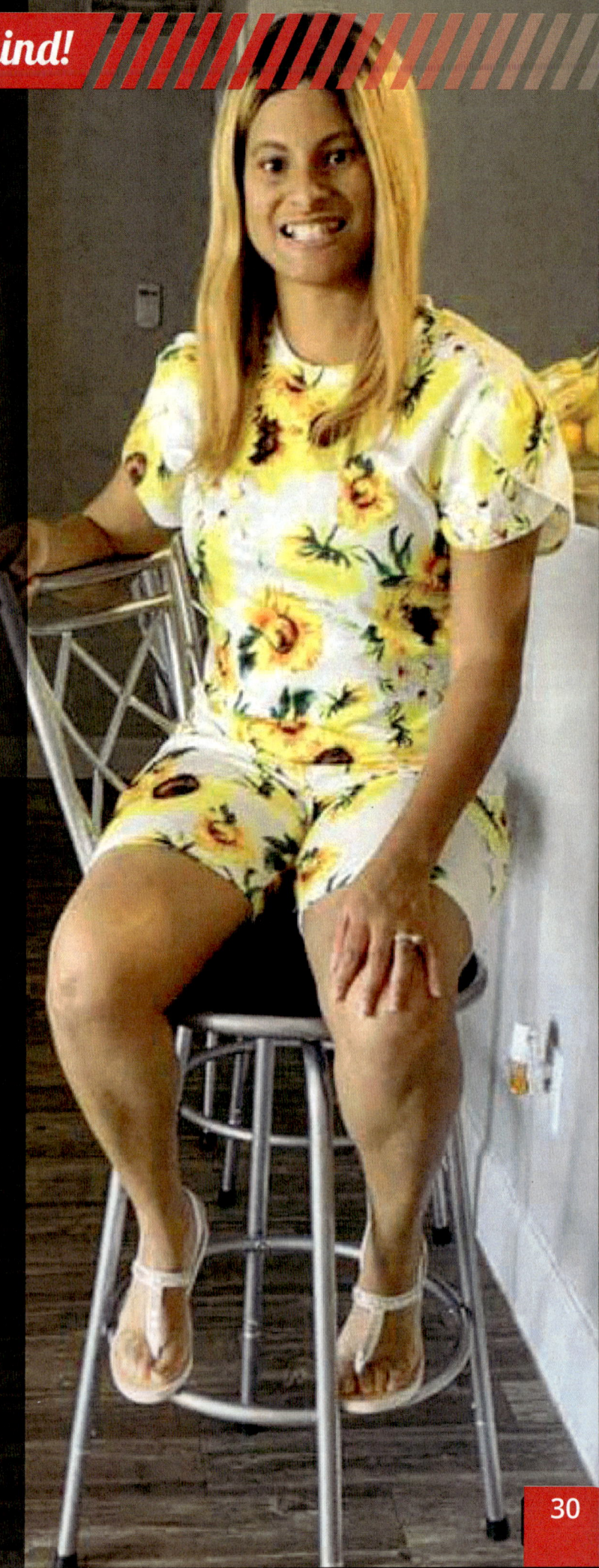

Rozina Jolla is a stay at home mom, wife, and business partner of Daniel Jolla III. As a homemaker, she still finds time to serve her community as a minister and worship leader of her local church as well as serve the community as a community organizer. With a strong passion for providing financial literacy, she has obtained financial licenses in several states across the US. Rozina is a rising financial coach and credit counselor specializing in evaluating each client by taking a holistic approach to analyzing the consumer's financial needs. We look to review ways to regulate cash flow, assist with credit restoration, assist with debt management, explore options for proper protection and wealth building.

SIS, YOU AIN'T SEEN NOTHING YET

According to statistics, 7 in 10 girls believe they are not good enough or do not measure up in some way, which includes their looks, performance in school, and relationships. That issue will cause an extreme confidence gap as girls become women, which means that experiences often cause women the confidence to decline. So from one sister to another, let me be the one to speak to your faith; awaken your courage, couture your character a little, and parade your charisma. One day I decided that despite my misfortunes, I was determined to change the trajectory of my life and as many others that would allow me to. Now, as a financial coach, I dedicate my time to helping families win the money game. Although I do not have a strong background in finance, I have managed to outwork the average person to equip myself with the knowledge to share with my family, my friends, my community, and any individual ready to change their lives for the better. What was my driving source, you ask? When I read that 8 out of 10 families live paycheck to paycheck. According to the federal reserve website,12 percent of adults would be unable to pay their current month's bills if they also had an unexpected $400 expense that they had to pay. I know we are currently in a pandemic, but Sis, even during a pandemic family, has begun to take steps toward financial freedom and creating generational wealth for their families. As you read this, you may be thinking to yourself that your net worth does not display any wealth at all. To your sister, I quote a very successful financial guru, Breanna McNeal, Looking like wealth does not mean you have already obtained it. It is the work you put in that matters. Looks come and eventually fade away. If we destroy generational curses of poverty by building women equipment with not only the strength, tenacity, beauty, and charisma you see on the outside, but with those qualities add a solid foundation of financial literacy, oh Sis, you have not seen anything yet.

According to statistics women, already make 90 percent of the household financial decisions. In fact, according to my readings, women will hold $110 trillion in assets by 2025. My question is, how much are you determined to contribute to that? Are you determine to take control of your money? How does your money work for you? How willing are you to be the curse breaker?

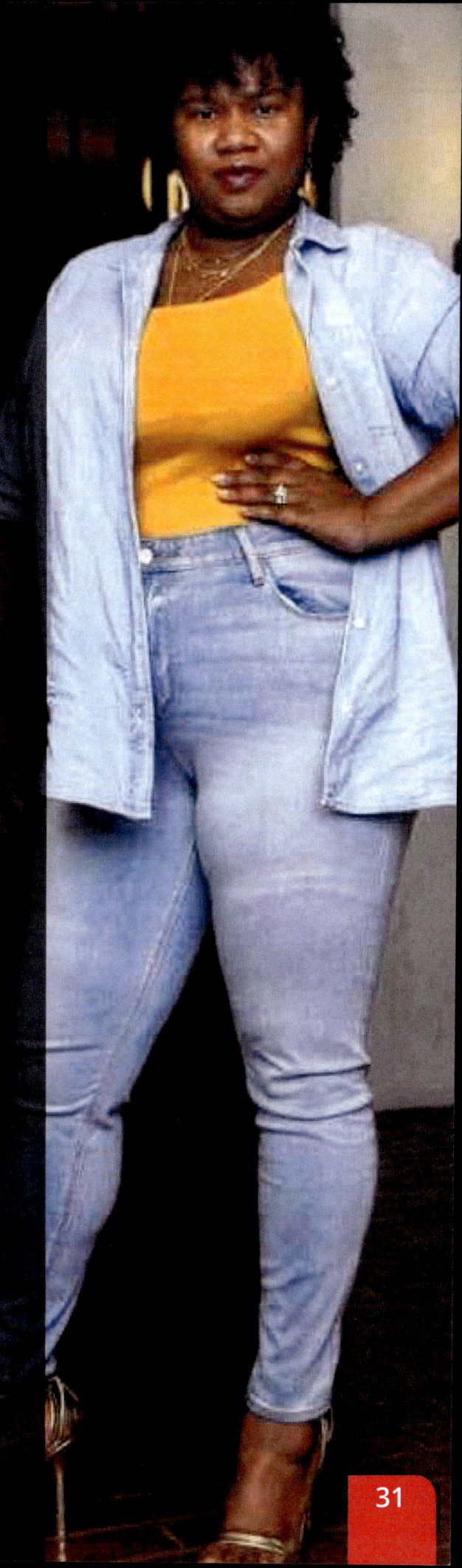

Tamara Faye is an accountant by trade with a heart for helping people learn from her mistakes to improve their personal finances. While successfully managing millions of dollars at work, Tamara's personal finances were a mess. The lightbulb went off one day that change needed to come and there has been no turning back ever since. Through both Tamara's personal and professional experiences, she helps women begin their journey toward securing a solid financial future for themselves and their families. Tamara Faye can be reached on Instagram and Twitter @TamaraFayeLLC or via email at **TamaraFayeConsulting@gmail.com**.

I Got Love All Over Me!

Loving Yourself through Your Relationship with Your Finances

There are many ways to express self-love, from spa days to sipping on your favorite beverage. One of the best is maintaining a good relationship with your finances. As someone who learned firsthand at the School of Hard Knocks, I have a few tips to share to help you get on track to a better relationship with your money and on the journey to building wealth.

1) Know your credit score and use credit wisely. Once you know your credit score, begin work on raising it, if needed, or protecting it. Simply put, putting that $600 pair of shoes on your credit card is a bad move.

2) Build an emergency fund. Several sources report anywhere from one-quarter to one-third of Americans have no emergency savings. Begin by consistently saving an amount you are comfortable with until you have $1,000 saved to cover unexpected expenses. Remember: those funds are for emergencies only and should be replenished ASAP after funding an emergency.

3) Learn the language of money. Compound interest, annual percentage yield and net worth sound like a foreign language until you learn what they mean. Spend some time learning the common money terms and what they mean to you.

4) Save for retirement. Whether you're 16 or 60, it is never too early or too late to start saving for retirement. Employer-sponsored plans are great if you have access to them. If not, research opening an Individual Retirement Account at a reputable bank.

5) Treat every major purchase as a business deal. Consider this: are you buying a home in an up and coming area or in an area seeing stagnant home values? When looking for a new car, will "new to you" do just fine? Analyze every large purchase in this way and watch how quickly your mindset will change.

There is no shame in making money mistakes, but as the saying goes, "When you know better, you do better." Some of us have had to learn the hard way how to be better stewards of our money. No matter where you are in your journey, the important thing is that you are on the journey. If you have not taken the dive into the pool of building a great relationship with your finances, use this year to do so. You have the power within you to chart a new financial course so get to it!

33

"I Got Love All Over Me"

Be the Queen of your romantic comeback. Be madly in love with the idea of being happy. One of Merriman-Webster's definition of love is an assurance of affection. It is also defined as a warm attachment, enthusiasm, or devotion. Valentine is defined as something, such as a movie or piece of writing; expressing uncritical praise or affection. There are multiple versions of the origin of Valentine's Day. One can conclude or summarize it is based on love, match making and even forbidden love and rituals. Has one considered this Holiday as an opportunity to outwardly love the most important person in your life? You.

One thing that has been revealed to me in recent days is the need to pour love into ourselves and to know that we are worthy of good love. The love that does not contradict actions. I am talking about that love that makes you feel warm all over. Why do we love others more than we do ourselves? Why don't we give ourselves credit, forgiveness and understanding? Maybe it is because we experienced hurt in the past. We beat ourselves up for even trusting the wrong people, places, and things. I challenge you this season to be open to love.

We were created to have the complete circle of the human experience this world has to offer. This place, this land and this earth is where we cultivate and create. We were created to feel all the human emotions. Let joy be your guide and trust the path that love takes you on. We were as vessels until our round-trip experience is complete. Love is a circle and in the center is "Self". Life is an assignment, an experience, and a journey. Embrace it, feel it, and enjoy it. Self-love is the true guide to living life abundantly which enables us to love others. In conclusion, love yourself so that you may completely love others. The reward is to be the happiness and security that is derived from loving yourself. Happy Valentine's Day and enjoy the poem.

I got love all over me
From my crown all the way down to my feet
When I look in the mirror, I am pleased with what I see
Filled with acceptance and peace
Wake-up in the morning and smile and purposefully be happy
Because the love inside us is natural healing

Temesha McCloud

A native of Akron, Ohio and mother of 4 has been writing poems, stories and self-help for over 10 years. A graduate of John R. Buchtel High School that also attended Bethune-Cookman University in Daytona Beach Florida as a freshman in college majoring in Business Administration. She also worked in the customer service industry for over 16 years and is also a Community Health Worker. She has been encouraging people with "Smile Cards" and Facebook Group "Release the bags". With the combination of the "Smile Cards" and "Release the bags" she encourages women and young ladies to free themselves from the past to be the best version on themselves. She is the founder of Encouragement Network and LadyBNCouraged. She can be found on Facebook as Temesha TA McCloud or Instagram as ladybncouraged_t.a.

I have took many of losses just to understand my purpose. I have been faced with many of obstacles that could have killed me. In only YHWH brought me through the battles. I often battle with myself not knowing if I was to enter into this world. In mostly all of the areas in my life I was trapped in the womb...needing a gasp for air. Feeling all alone where no one understood me. No one understood the pain that I was feeling inside physically, emotionally and mentally I was broken, damaged, wounded, scarred and bleeding internally. I was left to die at the moment of being trapped in the WOMB throughout my life. To be fearful of the obstacles, trials and tribulations throughout life it took me in different directions. I would often think to myself what is my reason for breathing? What's my reason for being born? I have no place here on this Earth. From the people that was supposed to love me unconditionally they were the same people that I feared. Broken as a little girl, trapped inside of the womb all I wanted was to live. For that little girl out there the feels trapped don't give up! The Lord is real,and He LOVES you. He sees the tears you cry... The LORD will never leave you nor forsake you. (Deuteronomy 31:6) "You have a PURPOSE!." "You are fearfully and wonderfully made in the image of God." (Psalms 139:141) "You are more than a conqueror through Jesus Christ that loves you." (Romans 8:37) "The Lord will make you the head and, not the tail." (Deuteronomy 28:13) little girl! "I will lift up my eyes unto the hills from within comes my help.... I looked up towards the mountain.. where does my help come from?" (Psalms 121:1) "I refuse to be TRAPPED." "Who the Son set free is free indeed." (John 8:34)

"I am a wife, mother of five beautiful children. A licensed childcare provider, and a Author."

#IREFUSETOLOSE

35

Timeless Wisdom
– Nomvula Rakolote

This is an extract form my book titled "Timeless Wisdom – Ndinguye Endinguye" (I AM that I AM [Exodus 3:14])
Why do we act surprised when things do not work out as anticipated or planned? Why do we think we can dictate how our lives unfold? Are we in charge or in control of our lives? Well, we may be in charge of certain aspects of our lives, but definitely not in control of our lives. If this is the case, what do we do? Where do we seek guidance?

Venturing into uncharted territories always yields solutions that are later referred to as 'tried and tested'. I have always had an understanding that nothing is new under the sun. I therefore pursued a relentless journey of trying to understand the source from which all the knowledge originates. I also know that we learn from experiences and lessons of others; and my question has always been: what and who directed them to find these solutions? Moreover, we end up benchmarking against past lessons and even apply those solutions to solve challenges of the present as if these are the only options that we have. We apply these lessons, whether or not they fit our circumstances or not, because we view and adopt them as the absolute truth.

I discovered that there is an extraordinary ingredient that we seldom acknowledge, even though it guides us irrespective. However, the difference is how we apply that ingredient in response to our life circumstances or situations. I am not sure how you would define this ingredient, but to me it is wisdom from God, and it is timeless because it has proven to transcend the only commodity that humanity is confined to, namely time. Hence King Solomon has affirmed that 'what has been will be again, what has been done will be done again...' (Ecclesiastes 1:9, NIV). In setting out to create the universe, God utilized wisdom as the basic principle of procedure.

Whatever You do, Seek Wisdom (Proverbs 4:7)
(the below is based on Proverbs 8 and cross-referenced)

I, WISDOM - MY ORIGIN

22 The Lord formed Me and brought Me forth at the beginning of His way, before His acts of old.
23 I was inaugurated and ordained from everlasting, from the beginning, before ever the earth existed (John 1:1).
30 Then I (Wisdom) was beside Him as a master and director of the work; and I was daily His delight, rejoicing before Him always, (John 1:2, 18).

I, WISDOM - WHERE TO FIND ME

12 I, Wisdom (from God), make prudence my dwelling, and I find out knowledge and discretion.
4 To you, O Men, I call, and my voice is directed to the sons of men.

I, WISDOM - MY ADVICE TO YOU

17 I love those that love me, and those who seek me early and diligently shall find me   (Ps. 91:14; John 14:21).

I, WISDOM - MY UNDERTAKING TO YOU

20 I walk in the way of righteousness.
15 By Me kings reign and rulers decree justice (Dan..2:21).
16 By Me princes' rule, and nobles, even all the judges and governors of the earth.

I, WISDOM - MY PARTING WORDS

35 For whoever finds Me finds life and draws forth and obtains favor from the Lord.
36 But he who misses me or sins against me wrongs and injures himself; all who hate me love and court death.

Affirmations

James 1:5-6 says, "If any of you lacks wisdom, you should ask God... But when you ask, you must believe and not doubt..." (NIV).

What I want
1. To seek and walk in the light of wisdom diligently (Proverbs 8: 17).
2. To seek godly wisdom because it is better than rubies, and is incomparable (Proverbs 8:11).
3. To guide me on when and how to speak and act.
4. For wisdom to mould my behaviour patterns and channel me to success in all my dealings (1 Samuel 18:14-16).
5. To not look for answers everywhere, but to seek wisdom, and not relegate it to the last resort.

My actions (I choose)
6. To be intentional, learn from my past, focus on the present and seek direction from God for the future.
7. To open my inner ears to receive wisdom into my inner being.
8. To obey and acknowledge that His wisdom is supreme.
9. To seek wisdom and understanding.

What I Promise
10. I am called, and therefore my eyes of understanding are enlightened (Ephesians 1:17-18).
11. I will hear God's instruction and be wise, and will not refuse it (Proverbs 8:33).
12. I will daily seek God for the spirit of wisdom and revelation (Ephesians 1:17-18).
13. I have access to the wisdom that transcends time and remains true to those that will dare to harness it in their lives.

I hope that you will join me in this journey of pursuing wisdom, which is fully explored in my book.

May this understanding be upon you and your children for generations to come. It is timeless, and it is for you to access freely!

Nomvula Rakolote
#POWEROFINTENT

Elder E. Deon Avery

Elder E. Deon Avery was born in Brevard, N.C., a little town outside of historic Asheville, N.C. Raised by her grandparents, the late John Robert and Mary Lou Gibbs, she learned very early the value of hard work, responsibility, and most importantly to have a relationship with God. An active member of Words of Deliverance Worldwide Ministries (WODWM) she serves on the Executive Council and as the Pastor of Finance. A firm believer that preparation is the key to success, Elder Deon has obtained her Bachelor's degree in Business Administration from Averett University and is currently pursuing her MBA Degree. Professionally, she has worked in the field of Accounting for over 20 years, with over 10 years in a management capacity.

Embracing the scripture "you intended to harm me, but God intended it for good to accomplish what is now being done, the saving of many lives", Behind the Mask Ministries was born.

While witnessing abuse throughout her childhood she ended up in abusive relationships in her adult life, where she encountered all forms of abuse. With an incredible story of overcoming decades of abuse and turning tragedy into victory, her focus on healing and restoration becomes real as she relates her personal story of abuse, battering, and even attempted suicide. Her prayer is that she can help others learn from her experiences, and not only shares valuable statistics, but also how to prevent becoming one. She is a soon to be author, committed to bringing awareness regarding abuse. It was her faith in God that gave her the resilience and strength to go on and has become her life mission to speak and educate others, that no matter what you have experienced, you CAN overcome your past, your past does not have to be your prison and that tragedy can in fact become your biggest triumph.

Second only to her personal relationship with God, Deon's greatest source of joy on earth are her three daughters, Kierra, Tiffany, and Jordan and her grandson Kameron.

When Forgiveness is All You Have

Sometimes life throws pebbles, stones, and even boulders at you. The question becomes, how will you respond? Will you become bitter or will you allow it to make you better? How many of us will take the issues of life and use it as ammunition to testify to a Genesis 50:20 lifestyle? In choosing to be better, I learned that walking in forgiveness personifies when the text says.... You intended to harm me, but God intended it for good to accomplish what is now being done, the saving of many lives (NIV). Forgiveness is not only a choice but it becomes a way of life.

From adolescence to adulthood, I experienced being abandoned, rejected, and abused financially, physically and verbally. The lack of forgiveness in my life caused negative feelings to manifest itself in the form of depression, attempted suicides, promiscuity, and an abundance of self-hate. All of which shaped who I was then, but when sifted through the lens of forgiveness, transformed into the motivation that has shaped who I have become.

When thinking about forgiveness, realize it is less about the people you considered to have mistreated you, and more about how you move forward in a productive, healthy life. Forgiveness is not overlooking, denying, excusing or ignoring what has happened. Forgiveness takes inventory of the hurt and damage, resolves what has happened, and declares control of your healing.

Choosing to say out loud what has happened can be helpful. If you can't say it out loud, write it down. The second step in forgiveness is forgiving yourself. Practice releasing the feelings of self-loathing until you become delivered from that mindset. Tell yourself, it is not your fault! No matter the circumstances, you cannot control other people and their actions. The last step in the forgiveness process is forgiving your offender. Oftentimes, people hurt, betray and mistreat others because they themselves have had similar experiences. At the point of your understanding, you can begin to forgive. Looking past the person's hurt to see the why, brings an absolution that cultivates peace in your mind, spirit and being.

Forgiveness is a daily practice that extends first from our heavenly Father and then from each and every one of us. I encourage you to search your hearts and find the courage and strength to SHOW forgiveness, to WALK in forgiveness, and to BE the example of what forgiveness looks like.

Social Media Handles

Facebook
https://www.facebook.com/Behindthemaskministries
Instagram
https://www.instagram.com/b_hindthemask/
Website
https://www.behindthemaskministries.com/

NEW LIFE
Global Church
SEEK. SAVE. SERVE.

Lisa Hawkins is a Pastor, Mentor, Advocate for Women, Prophetess, mother and grandmother. Lisa is a God-fearing woman of God, who loves the Lord with all her heart. Lisa was ordained and licensed as a pastor over 20 years ago and has continued to preach and teach the Word of God with power and demonstration. She is the daughter of Eunice Hawkins and a native of Mer. Rouge, La. She is currently the Founder and Pastor of New Life Global Church of Bastrop, La. Lisa is also the Chief Executive Officer of Lisa Hawkins Ministries which is a platform utilized to mentor and empower women who are called to minister the gospel. She is the former pastor of The True Vine BC in Oak Ridge, La and The Church that Makes A Difference of Bastrop, La.

Through Lisa Hawkins Ministries she has been afforded the opportunity to travel across the nation preaching, teaching, and proclaiming the Word of God. She has hosted numerous conferences, retreats, and Lisa also holds degrees in Business Administration and Business Technology. God has gifted her to move in the prophetic realm by the leading of the Holy Spirit. Pastor Lisa one desire is to see souls to saved, set free, and delivered.

Shayla Shaw is a Mental Wellness Advocate striving to end the stigma related to Mental Health. She is a dedicated wife, proud mother of four, and a very endearing grandmother. Shayla is a life coach devoted to mothers struggling with depressive behaviors that impair their abilities to be mentally and emotionally available to enjoy their families. Shayla is a suicide survivor. She was able to apply the experience, principles, and strategies she successfully utilized in her 15 years in Leadership as a Retail Operations Manager and certified as both a Project and Change Manager to develop a framework to thrive with her own Mental Illness. She now passionately pours herself into working with other mothers to ensure they are able to do the same with her "Emerging Mom" Program.

Shayla is a writer and her blog posts can be found at ShaylaShaw.com, being shared with her fellow members on the National Alliance on Mental Illness (nami.org), or The Mighty Site (themighty.com). She is also a member of The Project Management Institute, PMI Northern Louisiana Chapter, and the International Association of Women.

Shayla is the producer and host of the podcast, "Navigating My Crazy", that can be heard on all platforms including iTunes, Spotify, YouTube, Soundcloud, and Google Play. She created this podcast to inspire, share best practices, answer questions, speak with experts, and share real-life accounts of other mothers that are thriving as they battle depressive behaviors and balance life, family, and purpose. You can find resources, updates, sign up for sponsorships and advertisement, as well as listen to episodes on NavigatingMyCrazy.com.

Shayla is an entrepreneur. She is the owner of Her Eminence Sexe, where she creates organic and natural skin and body care products to ensure every woman feels like Royalty. (HerEminence.com). Her passion for increase financial literacy and breaking the cycles of poverty lead her to start Shaw Management & Estates' credit repair division to increase ownership and decrease debt in her community (TheShawEstates.com). Shayla is currently in the process of launching a nonprofit organization The Urban Youth Financial Literacy Foundation, UrFly.org, to empower disadvantaged youth with the skills and knowledge necessary to understand and manage financial resources to end the cycle of poverty.

You can keep up with all of Shayla's current events, send questions, episode request, book speaking engagements, and/or schedule a call at ShaylaShaw.com or email Shayla@shaylashaw.com. Like and follow all of Shayla's businesses on Facebook and Instagram.

Spotlight
with Real Talk Kingdom Ministries

Dr. Shirley Beckwith Mangum

Demetria Buie
demetriaministries.com
February 17, 2021
streamed on

the NOW network

www.thenownetwork.org

7pm ET / 4pm PT

BROADCAST TO **180 MILLION HOMES** IN SUB-SAHARAN AFRICA, WESTERN EUROPE & UNITED STATES

ON SATELLITE TV **INTELSAT**
LOCATED AT 68.5°E, IS-20

BROADCAST TO 56 MILLION HOMES ON CABLE TV IN UNITED STATES

42

Refuse To Lose

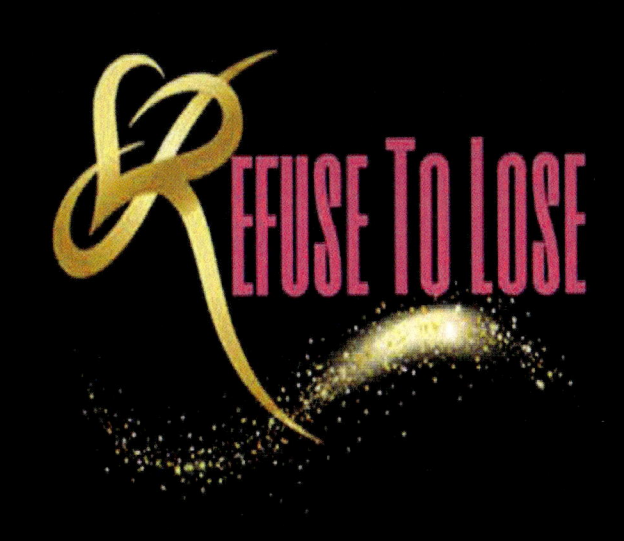

6 Black Entrepreneur WOMEN

Making A Change For The Future

ENTREPRENEUR

44

#Salvation. For God so loved the world that He gave His one and only Son, that whoever believes in Him shall not perish but have eternal life. For God did not send His Son into the world to condemn the world, but to save the world through Him.

SUBSCRIBE WITH US @ WWW.BUIEMAGAZINES.COM

Made in the USA
Columbia, SC
23 June 2022